5 MINUTE
HISTORY

DAVID WRAGG

FIRST WORLD WAR
AT SEA

First published 2014

The History Press
The Mill, Brimscombe Port
Stroud, Gloucestershire, GL5 2QG
www.thehistorypress.co.uk

© David Wragg, 2014

The right of David Wragg to be identified as the Author
of this work has been asserted in accordance with the
Copyright, Designs and Patents Act 1988.

British Library Cataloguing in Publication Data.
A catalogue record for this book is available from the British Library.

ISBN 978 0 7509 5567 6

Typesetting and origination by The History Press
Printed in Europe

CONTENTS

INTRODUCTION

THE ROYAL NAVY in 1914 was the largest in the world, mainly because for many years the service had adopted the so-called 'two-power standard', meaning that it had to be equal to the combined strength of any other two fleets in the world. The United States Navy was still developing, as was the German Navy (the *Kaiserliche Marine*), largely because Germany was itself a new creation and was just beginning to evolve from being a Continental power to possess greater ambitions.

Yet, all was not as it should have been. As big as it was, the Royal Navy was deployed around the globe protecting the largest empire the world had ever seen. Not for nothing did one of its admirals describe it as 'Weak everywhere, strong nowhere'. It had gone almost a century without major fleet actions and become more concerned with peacetime manoeuvres, and the initiative allowed to the commanding officers of warships in Nelson's day (especially smaller warships) had been suppressed.

Many in the Admiralty believed that experiment and innovation should be avoided. The Royal Navy had also been neglected by pre-war Liberal governments, allowing the United Kingdom's greatest rival in Europe – Germany – to begin to close the gap between the two navies.

On the other hand, the Royal Navy had not turned its back on progress. It had already adopted the submarine, and enthusiastic young officers were well to the fore in learning to fly and experiment with the aeroplane. The Royal Navy was quick to embrace the steam turbine, which not only provided more power than piston steam engines, but lowered the height of the engine room, allowing heavier armament and armour. This led to the first all-big-gun battleship, HMS *Dreadnought*, completed in 1906. From that year onwards, all battleships were classified as being either 'Dreadnought' or 'pre-Dreadnought'. The problem that this gave the Royal Navy was that overnight its lead in major warships was cancelled out and a race began to see which country could build the most Dreadnought battleships before war broke out in Europe. The Imperial German Navy received its first Dreadnought battleship in 1907 – a sign of what was to come.

THE ROYAL NAVY IN 1914

IN OCTOBER 1904, Admiral Sir John Fisher became First Sea Lord, the service head of the Royal Navy, while the political head was the First Lord of the Admiralty. The Second Sea Lord was responsible for personnel and the Third Sea Lord was Controller of the Navy and responsible for warship design and support. Fisher had held both these posts earlier in his career.

Fisher was one of the great reforming admirals. He was what today would be described as a 'technocrat', rather than a fighting admiral, although he was no engineer and at the time engineers were treated with disdain, despite half a century of steam power. A controversial figure, Fisher incurred the wrath of many senior officers by bringing home from the various fleets, squadrons and overseas stations many older ships, which, in his words, 'could neither fight nor run away'. Many of the ships already at home and in reserve were in a similar condition and were scrapped. His predecessors had kept as many ships as possible, confusing sheer numbers with efficiency and having a fleet that had quantity rather than quality.

It was very much a spit and polish navy. Smartness and cleanliness were more highly regarded than fighting efficiency; one battleship's watertight doors had been polished so much that they were too thin to be effective.

Gunnery practise was neglected because it made the ships dirty and it was not unknown for practice munitions to be quietly dumped over the side.

Yet, ships could not avoid becoming dirty when they had to recoal, which took some time as a battleship required some 3,000–3,500 tons of coal, loaded largely by hand, apart from a hoist lifting the coal out of a barge or collier. Working together, the ship's company could handle some 300 tons per hour. Coaling was necessary every seven to ten days, with HMS *Dreadnought*, regarded as being economical, needing 300 tons of coal daily. Of course, oil would have been a more efficient fuel and much easier to refuel, but the United Kingdom had scant oil resources, whereas coal was abundant. The new Queen Elizabeth-class battleships were amongst the first to be oil-fired from the start.

In 1914, the Royal Navy had 147,667 men, but mobilisation raised this to just over 201,000,

---

DID YOU KNOW?

The contract for supplying the oil needed by the Royal Navy was awarded to British Petroleum (BP) in return for the state taking a half-share in the company.

I WAS THERE

Painting the ship's sides and superstructure was an evolution that usually had to be done in a day. With one captain it would be every six or seven weeks, with another every six months ... Every brush you lost, you paid for. So you hung them round your neck.

James Cox, a pre-1914 naval rating[1]

and by 1917 the number had risen to 450,000. By 1918, it also had 7,000 women in the newly formed Women's Royal Naval Service (WRNS), more commonly known as the 'Wrens'.

At the outbreak of the First World War, the Royal Navy had sixty-nine capital ships: twenty Dreadnought and forty pre-Dreadnought battleships and nine battlecruisers. It also had forty-six cruisers and sixty-two light cruisers, twenty-eight gunboats, eleven sloops, 215 torpedo-boat destroyers, 106 torpedo boats, seventy-six submarines, a seaplane carrier and seven small minelayers. The light cruisers were no bigger than a Second World War destroyer, while the torpedo-boat destroyers, of less than 1,000 tons displacement, were the predecessors of the much larger modern destroyer. Despite its size, the Royal Navy lacked minelayers, minesweepers, night gunnery systems, anti-

DID YOU KNOW?

One of the ships used for pre-war trials with seaplanes was a light cruiser, HMS *Hermes*, but she was converted back on the outbreak of war and all wartime seaplane carriers were converted merchant vessels.

I WAS THERE

We get up at 6.30, and have to take our dip in the plunge bath and dress by 7.00, when we begin work till 8.00. At 8.00 the bugle blows 'Cease Fire' and we are marched into the mess room. At 9.00 we have prayers and divisions (that is, fall in) and off we march to work, which varies …

Douglas King-Harman, an officer cadet at Osborne, aged 12 ½ years[2]

airship weapons, anti-submarine equipment and tactics, efficient torpedoes and safe harbours.

The main naval bases were at Chatham (sometimes referred to as the Nore Command), Portsmouth and Plymouth. There were historical reasons for the location of these, as wars had been fought against the Spanish, French and the Dutch. However, as war with Germany grew more likely, a new base was started at Rosyth, on the north bank of the Firth of Forth, but progress was slow, as many senior officers thought the location too far from the open sea. Locating a base further north was difficult as the railway lines to the north of Scotland were single-track. Nevertheless, a forward base was built at Invergordon on the Cromarty Firth, north of Inverness, which was provided with a floating dock. Further north still, an anchorage was created at Scapa Flow, off the mainland of Orkney, which had to be resupplied by sea. A shortage of funds further delayed the completion of these bases.

The largest force in the Royal Navy was the Home Fleet, with its bases in the south of England, while there was also the Atlantic Fleet based in Gibraltar, the Mediterranean Fleet based in Malta, the China Squadron based in Hong Kong, the East Indies Station at Singapore and the North American and West

Indies Station at Bermuda. There was also an Australian Squadron.

Impressive though this spread of warships might be, Admiral Lord 'Jacky' Fisher maintained that away from home waters, the Royal Navy was still very weak.

The Home Fleet consisted of a First Fleet with three squadrons of Dreadnought battleships manned by regular personnel, a Second Fleet of two pre-Dreadnought battleship squadrons, which when mobilised would be manned by personnel from the naval schools, and a Third Fleet manned by skeleton maintenance or core crews, but dependent on reservists for operations. The First Fleet alone was stronger than the German Navy.

On the outbreak of war, the Home Fleet's sub-fleets came together to form the Grand Fleet.

THE IMPERIAL GERMAN NAVY IN 1914

PRIOR TO UNIFICATION in 1872, Germany was a collection of states, of which the strongest and most important was Prussia, which already had a navy that formed the basis of the new *Kaiserliche Marine*, or Imperial German Navy. At first, Germany was content to view itself simply as a Continental power. The senior service was the army, but in 1900 the Kaiser decreed that both services had equal status. Earlier, in 1898, a Naval Act had authorised the construction of a substantial German navy.

While the new state had far-flung ambitions and wanted its own empire to rival those, in particular, of the United Kingdom and France, one problem was the short length of coastline outside the confines of the Baltic Sea. This meant that ships sailing to and from Germany had to use the confined and shallow waters of the Kattegat and Skagerrak. Therefore, between 1887 and 1895, the Kiel Canal was constructed so that shipping, and especially warships, could navigate between the North Sea and the Baltic in any weather and at all states of the tide.

In 1906, a programme to widen the Kiel Canal began and was completed in August 1914, just in time for the start of hostilities. German ambitions were also helped by the UK ceding the island of Heligoland to Germany in 1890.

DID YOU KNOW?

In 1910, the parental contribution for a German cadet officer was 1,505 marks for the first year, some 200 marks above the average industrial wage, and 1,000 marks for the following three years, after which it was 600 marks as an annual allowance for four years so that a junior lieutenant could maintain the lifestyle expected of an officer.

Had it remained in British hands, the island could have provided a base for light forces and aircraft to attack Germany and German shipping. Also in 1906, HMS *Dreadnought* was launched, making all other battleships obsolete. Overnight, British naval superiority was lost, as a race got under way to see which country could build the largest number of battleships before the start of hostilities.

Kaiser Wilhelm II, who came to the throne in 1888, was determined to create a navy that was the equal of the Royal Navy, an ambition that was shared by his Secretary for the Navy, Admiral Tirpitz. German naval expansion was viewed with alarm by many in the UK, especially as Germany had its first Dreadnought-standard battleships by 1907 and was improving her shipbuilding capabilities,

I WAS THERE

The whole [German] Navy without exception are absolutely devoted to HM [the Kaiser], not only as their Emperor but also particularly in a personal sense.

Report by the British naval attaché in Berlin, 1910[3]

as well as other important aspects such as heavy gun production. The first Dreadnought battlecruisers were in service with the Royal Navy by 1907 and with the Imperial German Navy by 1910.

In 1914, the Imperial German Navy had seventeen Dreadnought-standard battleships and seven Dreadnought-standard battlecruisers. By this time, it was the second largest navy in the world, ahead of the United States and Japan, but still behind the Royal Navy. In addition to its Dreadnoughts, it had another twenty pre-Dreadnought battleships, seven modern light cruisers and eighteen older ships, as well as thirty submarines with petrol engines and another ten with the more efficient and much safer diesel engines, while another seventeen were building.

It was not just a case of raw numbers of ships. German investment in gun production and in developing superior guns meant that an 11in gun aboard a German ship could fire twenty-four shells, or rounds, a minute, compared to sixteen shells a minute from the British 12in guns. The British 12in gun would have a slightly longer range than the German 11in gun, and would also pack a bigger punch. On the other hand, the Germans had far superior optical technology that meant that they had far better range-finders and night-fighting equipment than the British, even though they did not have a director-firing system.

The other important aspect of German naval power was its use of airships, the large Zeppelin dirigibles. These were, at first, far superior to any bomber fielded by the British, but were vulnerable to fire from British warships. They were, nevertheless, able to attack British towns and cities while the Royal Navy was limited in its ability to attack German cities, although it did send seaplanes against Zeppelin bases.

German naval ratings were far less experienced than their British counterparts, signing on for three years, while in the Royal Navy twelve years was the minimum. Officers did not usually assist in coaling ships and flogging was still practised, having been abolished in the Royal Navy in the nineteenth century.

DID YOU KNOW?

Although retired from the Royal Navy, the former First Sea Lord, Admiral of the Fleet Lord Fisher, was able to calculate virtually the date of war breaking out by using estimates for the completion of widening the Kiel Canal.

July
28

I WAS THERE

His first question, which he put to me without knowing what I wanted of him at such an early morning hour, was: 'Would England take part in the coming war or not?'

Karl Dönitz, Signals Officer of the cruiser Breslau, on meeting the German consul in Brindisi*

ALLIED NAVAL STRATEGY

FOR THE NAVAL officers of the period, war at sea meant looking for a major naval engagement. The great British victory against the French at Trafalgar in 1805 cast a shadow over officers of all ranks, and Nelson was regarded as the model for captains and admirals. There had been only three major naval engagements between steamships: the Battle of the Yellow Sea and the Battle of the Japanese Sea, both in August 1904; and the Battle of Tsushima, in May 1905. However, the Royal Navy had not been involved in them, as these were major engagements in the Russo–Japanese war of 1904–05.

The Allies, or Entente Powers, consisted of the United Kingdom and France, joined by Italy and, later, Japan. The Royal Navy was stronger than the Imperial German Navy. While Germany was the main opponent, France and Italy had to counter the Austro-Hungarians in the Adriatic and Mediterranean, with Turkey allied with Germany in the Mediterranean. Germany and the Austro-Hungarian Empire comprised the Central Powers.

British naval strategy was the key to that of the Entente's. The framework of the country's naval strategy was largely that of one man, Admiral of the Fleet Lord 'Jackie' Fisher, who had become First Sea Lord in October 1904, and remained in post until January 1910.

DID YOU KNOW?

In 1914, Germany had a far larger merchant fleet than today, totalling 5.5 million tons or 12 per cent of the world total. After 5 August 1914, the British moved quickly to seize German and Austrian vessels, with 623 German and 101 Austrian ships in neutral harbours, while 675,000 tons of the Central Powers' shipping was seized and another 405,000 tons captured on the high seas so that within weeks the operational German merchant fleet was down to just 2 million tons.

Fisher believed that there were 'five strategic keys to the empire and world economic system: Gibraltar, Alexandria and Suez, the Cape of Good Hope, and the Straits of Dover', and saw his role as keeping control of them all. He also believed that the German Navy never fought more than a few hours from its home ports, and that the Royal Navy's fighting ground should also be its training ground, meaning the North Sea.

A somewhat similar view was taken by Admiral John Jellicoe, sent from the Admiralty on the outbreak of war to take command of the Grand Fleet. On 30 October, he wrote to the Admiralty testing his strategy, which was to confront the Germans in the northern North

Sea rather than the southern, as the latter would favour the Germans, who would be able to deploy minelayers and submarines. The problem would arise when, in chasing retreating German forces, the Grand Fleet ran into a chain of submarines.

Where Jellicoe broke ranks with many of his peers was that he believed that retaining control of the seas was more important than engaging the enemy. One reason for this was that he did not want to lose any of his major fleet units, battleships and battlecruisers, but instead keep the Royal Navy's overwhelming dominance intact. This was essential to enforce the blockade of German ports.

The importance of the blockade meant that the war on land benefitted as well as the war at sea. Before the First World War, Germany imported around a quarter of its food, as well as half of its animal fodder. Much of the food and animal fodder was supplied by Russia, a source that would dry up as soon as war began. Although self-sufficient in some items, such as potatoes, the country was heavily dependent on fertilisers, half of which came from North America or North Africa, which were vital for crops to grow in the sandy soils of northern Germany. Germany relied on the United States for all of its cotton and for 60 per cent of its copper.

I WAS THERE

In the middle of coaling the ship this evening, the Admiral ... made a general signal that 'Hostilities with Germany commence at midnight'. So we are in for it.

Sub Lieutenant Douglas King-Harman, letter dated 4 August 1914[5]

DID YOU KNOW?

Although Germany was not a maritime power, it was heavily dependent on imports for both the economy to function and the people to survive.

The German response to the blockade was to use neutral ships to sail to ports in neutral nations such as the Netherlands, Denmark and Norway. Cargoes could be unloaded and moved by railway or coastal shipping, or, in the case of cargo, unloaded at Rotterdam and moved inland by barge. Goods landed in Norway could be taken by railway to Sweden. Between 1913 and 1914, imports to Germany from Sweden, or perhaps more accurately *via* Sweden, rose from US $2.2 million to US $17.7 million, with similar increases in trade between the Netherlands and Denmark and Germany.

If the enemy would not come out to sea and fight, then the next measure was to bombard its coastal positions. The short length of the German North Sea coastline did not make this a cost-effective option, but at Gallipoli British and French warships bombarded Turkish forts and even attempted, at some cost, to enter the Dardanelles – the channel between the Gallipoli Peninsula and Asiatic Turkey or Anatolia.

There were also raids on the German-held ports of Ostend and Zeebrugge, using blockships and troops to close these for enemy use.

The Royal Navy managed with some difficulty and much skill and courage on the part of its submarine commanders to send submarines into both the Baltic Sea and the Bosporus, where they inflicted much damage, although operations in the Baltic were gradually reduced as the Russian Revolution saw bases lost to the Bolsheviks, who had concluded a peace with the Germans.

In view of the successful submarine operations by the Royal Navy in these two enclosed seas, one marked oversight in the maritime strategy was the failure to institute a convoy system until the last year of the war, when it was, to some extent, insisted upon by the United States Navy. Part of the problem was that anti-submarine warfare was in its infancy and sonar did not appear until almost the end of the war, while hydrophones were affected by the machinery and propeller noise of the submarine-hunting vessel. Nevertheless, the Germans were having considerable success with surface raiders and Allied merchant shipping losses were so immense that the United Kingdom was itself in danger of starvation.

KEY FIGURES OF
THE NAVAL WAR

THE GERMAN ARCHITECT of the wartime Imperial German Army was *Grossadmiral* (Grand Admiral, equivalent of Admiral of the Fleet) Alfred von Tirpitz, who was Secretary of State from 1897 until his dismissal in 1916, while his British counterpart was Admiral of the Fleet Lord 'Jackie' Fisher, who was First Sea Lord from 1904 to 1910, but recalled to the Admiralty by Winston Churchill in October 1914. Beneath these two men were the Grand Fleet's Jellicoe and Beatty and the High Seas Fleet's Scheer and Hipper.

FISHER

As First Sea Lord, the service head of the Royal Navy, from 1904 to 1910, Admiral of the Fleet Lord 'Jackie' Fisher is best known for commissioning HMS *Dreadnought*, the first 'all-big-gun' battleship completed in 1906. He attracted much opposition for bringing home much of the Royal Navy's widely dispersed fleet of older ships that 'could neither fight nor run away'.

Fisher retired amidst great controversy and rivalry with another senior officer. In retirement, he endeavoured to make it easier for non-commissioned personnel in the Royal Navy and Royal Marines to achieve commissioned rank. Recalled to the Admiralty by Winston

Churchill, the First Sea Lord (the political head of the Royal Navy), in October 1914, he proposed shortening the war by recommending landings in the Baltic for a march on Berlin, and at Gallipoli to seize the peninsula. The two men proved incompatible, and in May 1915, Fisher walked out of the Admiralty, and returned to retirement until his death in 1920.

DID YOU KNOW?

German and British battlecruisers were almost the exact opposite. The British ships had battleship-calibre guns but sacrificed armour plating for high speed, while the German counterparts were heavily armoured but used lower calibre guns.

JELLICOE

Admiral Sir John Jellicoe, later Admiral of the Fleet Viscount Jellicoe of Scapa, was appointed commander of the Grand Fleet on 4 August 1914 by the First Sea Lord, Winston Churchill.

Jellicoe saw his duty as maintaining a strong fleet rather than seeking a major engagement with the Germans in which many ships would be lost. Nevertheless, his prompt action in putting to sea before the Battle of Jutland in 1916 meant that his ships avoided a trap involving German submarines. Although Jutland was a tactical victory for the Germans, who suffered far fewer losses in men and ships, it was a strategic victory for the British, as the Grand Fleet did not venture to sea in strength afterwards. However, it was still regarded as a big disappointment by the British public, who had expected a major victory on the scale of Trafalgar.

Jellicoe was promoted to First Sea Lord in November 1916, at a time when the German U-boat campaign was at its peak. He resolutely refused to organise a convoy system and during his spell in office the UK came close to starvation. In 1917, he was dismissed by a new First Lord of the Admiralty, Sir Eric Geddes, but was promoted to Admiral of the Fleet in 1919. Later he became Earl Jellicoe. He died in London in 1935 from pneumonia.

BEATTY

At Jutland, Vice Admiral David Beatty was commander of the 1st Battlecruiser Squadron, the vanguard of the Grand Fleet. Beatty's role was to draw the enemy out and keep his superior, the commander-in-chief of the Grand Fleet, Admiral Sir John Jellicoe, informed of the enemy's position. He was successful in the first, but failed miserably in the second.

At Jutland he became famous for his remark to his flag captain, Ernle Chatfield, later a First Sea Lord: 'There seems to be something wrong with our bloody ships today.' This was after two of his battlecruisers exploded with tremendous loss of life within half-an-hour.

He relieved Jellicoe as commander of the Grand Fleet in late 1916 and in this role he was later able to escort the German High Seas Fleet to internment at Scapa Flow.

Beatty retired in 1927. Unwell and advised by his doctor to remain in bed, he nevertheless rose to act as a pallbearer at Jellicoe's funeral in 1935, catching a chill that led to his death.

TIRPITZ

Grand Admiral Alfred von Tirpitz headed the Imperial German Navy from 1897 to 1916. None of the states that came together to form a united Germany in 1871 had been a maritime power, but Kaiser Wilhelm II, who came to the throne in 1888, decreed that the German Navy was to be on an equal footing with the army, which had been the senior service.

By 1914, the Imperial German Navy was the second largest in the world. Tirpitz believed that if the Germans possessed a navy of sufficient strength, the British would try to avoid confrontation because of the risk of losing naval dominance in any battle.

DID YOU KNOW?

The destroyer had evolved from the torpedo-boat destroyer, a small fast ship intended to counter the growing menace of the torpedo boat, itself a fast lightly armed warship. From the late nineteenth century onwards, the major navies were obsessed by the damage they believed could be inflicted by torpedo boats.

Tirpitz's strategy was one of minor engagements, aided by mining off the British North Sea ports and using submarine warfare to inflict damage on British overseas trade. This last aspect of his naval strategy was controversial after the sinking of the liner *Lusitania*, which caused the Kaiser to fear that the USA might enter the war on the side of the Allies. The Imperial German Navy also made extensive use of commerce raiders, usually converted merchant ships, and these ranged far and wide, including the Pacific.

To avoid drawing the USA into the war, the Kaiser forbade unrestricted U-boat warfare. This ran counter to Tirpitz's strategy and he felt compelled to resign as relations between the two men deteriorated.

He died in Ebenhausen, near Munich, in March 1930.

SCHEER

Admiral Reinhard Scheer took command of the German High Seas Fleet early in 1916. A strict disciplinarian, he was known as the 'man with the iron mask' by his subordinates.

He was the author of *Guiding Principles for Warfare in the North Sea*, which outlined his strategy for naval warfare. A believer in aggressive tactics, Scheer believed that heavy bombardments of the east coast of England should be used to lure out the Royal Navy, which could then be engaged in a series of battles that would gradually erode its numerical superiority before confronting the Grand Fleet, which was to be subjected to constant attack and harassment by U-boats and Zeppelin airships.

Like Tirpitz, Scheer believed in unrestricted submarine warfare. When the Kaiser banned this, he ordered all the U-boats back to Germany and reassigned them to patrols off British ports. Here they were to attack British warships that were leaving the ports, after counter-attacks by German warships on British coastal towns.

Post-Jutland he urged unrestricted submarine warfare, lobbying so vigorously for this that the restrictions were lifted in 1917.

After the war, he wrote his autobiography *Vom Segelschiff zum U-Boot* (*From Sailing Ship to Submarine*), and was preparing to meet Jellicoe when he died in 1928 at Weimar at the age of 65 years.

I WAS THERE

I had to find myself another flagship because I could no longer exercise command from one which was shot to pieces ... A torpedo boat was called alongside and we changed under heavy fire ... I drove my torpedo boat hoping to find an advantageous moment to board another battlecruiser. These 1½ hours that I spent in a hail of shell and splinters aboard the torpedo boat I shall not be likely to forget.

Vice Admiral von Hipper on his transfer from the crippled Lutzow to the Moltke, at the height of the Battle of Jutland, 1916

HIPPER

Franz von Hipper was Scheer's successor as the commander of the German High Seas Fleet. His fame rests on his role as commander of the German battlecruisers at the Battle of Jutland, when he was a *vizeadmiral*, or vice admiral. By the time of Jutland he was already notorious for taking his battlecruisers on raids of English coastal towns, for which he was known as the 'baby killer'.

At Jutland, his battlecruisers engaged Beatty's in a running battle in which his flagship *Lützow* was so badly damaged that he had to transfer his command to *Moltke*. This was not an easy task in the middle of a battle, and he spent almost two hours in a torpedo boat making the transfer.

In command of the High Seas Fleet afterwards, he planned a major attack on the Thames Estuary, but this failed to materialise as German sailors began to desert en masse, while others mutinied.

Hipper died in 1932 aged 68.

NAVAL HEROES

AS IN ANY war, both sides had their heroes, but the British had more because the Royal Navy possessed ships of all kinds at sea, from the beginning to the end, and was engaged in action around the world. As a sign of what was to come, the heroes included submariners and aviators.

THE BRITISH HEROES

This is a selection of the Royal Navy personnel who were awarded the Victoria Cross (VC), Britain's highest decoration.

Squadron Commander Richard Frederick Bell Davies

In company with Flying Sub Lieutenant Gilbert Smylie, Bell Davies was sent to bomb Ferrijik Junction, Thrace, north-west of Gallipoli, in November 1915. Both aircraft carried six 20lb bombs, but Smylie's aircraft was hit and the engine failed, leaving him to glide over the target and drop five of his bombs. He made an emergency landing on a mudbank and set his aircraft alight to prevent it falling into enemy hands. Smylie then saw Bell Davies circling, preparing to land, unaware of the unexploded bomb, so Smylie shot at the bomb, causing it to explode. Bell Davies then landed and rescued Smylie, both men returning safely to their squadron.

Bell Davies also flew reconnaissance flights over the Dardanelles and later was present at Jutland.

John 'Jack' Cornwell

At Jutland, the light cruiser HMS *Chester* was outgunned in action against four German light cruisers. Within minutes it was hit seventeen times, losing fire control and resulting in the deaths of thirty men, with forty-six wounded, including the crew of the forward 5.5in turret. One member of the gun crew remained alive – mortally wounded Boy, Second Class, John Travers Cornwell (commonly known as Jack), the sight setter, who remained at his post awaiting orders. He died in hospital in Grimsby on 2 June 1916.

Major Francis Harvey

Major Francis Harvey, Royal Marine Light Infantry, commanded the marines aboard the battlecruiser *Lion* at Jutland. The ship was hit amidships on Q turret, killing the crew and starting a fire. Mortally wounded, Harvey ordered the magazine doors to be closed and then flooded to prevent it exploding, and so, despite the fire igniting the cordite in the turret area killing every man there, the ship was saved.

Lieutenant Commander Martin Eric Nasmith

Ordered by Commodore (Submarines) Roger Keyes to 'Go and run amuck in the Marmara', Nasmith obeyed and took his submarine *E11*. Getting into the Sea of Marmara through the narrow and often shallow channel of the Dardanelles was difficult enough, but once there the damage Nasmith inflicted on Turkish shipping was such that the Turks were convinced a flotilla of submarines was present. *E11* sank a large gunboat, an ammunition ship, three store ships and two transports, as well as a large troop-carrying barge and three minor vessels. Nasmith also has the accolade of taking the first photographs through a submarine periscope.

Flying Sub Lieutenant Reginald John Warneford

Warneford was the first Royal Naval Air Service pilot to shoot down a Zeppelin after a running battle with *LZ-37* north of Ostend. The Zeppelin crashed into flames on the roof of a convent, killing two nuns and two orphans, while Warneford had to land to make repairs to his Morane-Saulnier parasol monoplane. He shot the Zeppelin down on 7 June 1915 and received the official citation on 11 June, the shortest interval between deed and award in the history of the Victoria Cross.

THE GERMAN HEROES

The scope for heroism in the Imperial German Navy was largely with the submariners or commerce raiders.

Captain Lieutenant Felix Graf von Luckner

A former merchant navy officer, Luckner was called up in 1912 and initially served in a gunboat. Luckner was given command of the former *Pass of Balmaha*, a three-masted sailing ship converted to a commerce raider, with concealed 105mm guns and two auxiliary engines and renamed *Seeadler* (*Sea Eagle*). On 21 December 1916, she left port on a long cruise, during which no less than fourteen Allied merchantmen were captured. Most of the men, including Luckner himself, could speak Norwegian, in case the ship was boarded by a British warship, and in fact she slipped through the blockade disguised as a Norwegian ship. On Christmas Day, when south-east of Iceland, the British armed merchant cruiser HMS *Avenger* boarded her, but did not discover that she was an armed German ship. Luckner became known as *Der Seeteufel* (the Sea Devil) – and his crew *Die Piraten des Kaiser* (the Kaiser's pirates).

Luckner's ship would approach an Allied merchant vessel requesting the time – something that was not uncommon for a sailing ship – and, having got within range, would raise the German naval ensign, expose his guns and fire shots to encourage the ship's master to surrender. This was so successful that Luckner's entire cruise did not cause any Allied casualties. After boarding the ships and taking the crews prisoner, the ships were scuttled. Once, a captured merchant ship was taken into Rio de Janeiro to obtain more supplies for *Seeadler*, before being scuttled afterwards. In March 1917, a ship was captured, but instead of scuttling her, Luckner transferred his prisoners and set the ship free to reach the nearest port. Luckner escaped being caught in a trap set by the Royal Navy and on learning that the United States had entered the war, started to seize US ships.

On 24 August, *Seeadler* was wrecked on the edge of a lagoon on the island of Mopelia. Fortunately, the ship's boats survived the wreck, so Luckner was able to take one and he sailed almost 2,500 miles across the Pacific, calling at the Society Islands and Fiji, before seizing another ship. However, this was wrecked and he was eventually taken prisoner. Despite an attempt at escape, he spent the rest of the war in New Zealand POW camps.

U-boat Commanders

These are the ten most successful U-boat commanders of the war, who sunk a combined total of 1,726 ships, amounting to 3,992,284 tons of shipping:

1. Lothar von Arnauld de la Perière
   195 ships sunk or captured (455,869 tons)
   8 ships damaged (34,312 tons)

2. Walther Forstmann
   149 ships sunk or captured (391,607 tons)
   7 ships damaged (30,552 tons)

3. Max Valentiner
   144 ships sunk or captured (299,474 tons)
   6 ships damaged (33,151 tons)

4. Otto Steinbrinck
   206 ships sunk or captured (244,797 tons)
   12 ships damaged (65,720 tons)

5. Hans Rose
   82 ships sunk or captured (221,942 tons)
   9 ships damaged (45,606 tons)

6. Gustav Sieß
   56 ships sunk or captured (188,295 tons)
   10 ships damaged (36,363 tons)

7. Walther Schwieger
   49 ships sunk or captured (185,212 tons)
   4 ships damaged (3,488 tons)

8. Wolfgang Steinbauer
   51 ships sunk or captured (183,871 tons)
   12 ships damaged (60,480 tons)

9. Claus Rücker
   80 ships sunk or captured (174,655 tons)
   3 ships damaged (9,951 tons)

10. Reinhold Saltzwedel
    111 ships sunk or captured (172,768 tons)
    10 ships damaged (17,131 tons)

HELIGOLAND BIGHT
AND DOGGER BANK

THE FIRST MAJOR naval action of the war occurred off Heligoland Bight on 28 August 1914, in the same month that war was declared. The island of Heligoland had been British territory, but had been ceded to Germany in 1890 by the British Government in exchange for the island of Zanzibar, off the coast of East Africa. While some senior officers advocated seizing the island prior to an invasion of Germany, it was some 30 miles off the German coast. It is a moot point whether the island was more valuable in British hands than Zanzibar, as in wartime it would have required a sizeable garrison to prevent German seizure and resupply would have been difficult given its relatively close proximity to Germany.

At first light on a misty morning, a force of British cruisers and destroyers approached the area and started to attack German destroyers, sinking one of them. As the action continued, German light cruisers joined the fight, damaging the British light cruiser *Arethusa* and several destroyers. Steaming to the rescue was Rear Admiral Beatty's battlecruiser squadron, with Beatty in his flagship HMS *Lion* and accompanied by *Queen Mary*, *Princess Royal*, *Invincible* and *New Zealand*, as well as eight cruisers and a number of destroyers. Within a few minutes of opening fire, Beatty's ships had sunk the German light cruisers *Ariadne*, *Koln* and *Mainz*. The German battlecruiser squadron left port too late and arrived after the British ships had withdrawn.

The Dogger Bank is an extensive sandbank about 100 miles off the coast of Northumberland. For centuries it was famous as a fishing ground, especially for cod, but the First World War was to add its name to the long list of naval battles.

It was fishing trawlers that *Konteradmiral* (Rear Admiral) Franz von Hipper was seeking on 24 January 1915, as well as British light forces. The interest in the trawlers was because the Germans suspected them of acting as an early warning for the Royal Navy, although at this time few, if any, had wireless. Hipper's battlecruiser squadron consisted of his flagship, *Seydlitz*, the *Derfflinger* and the *Moltke*, as well as the armoured cruiser *Blücher* and four light cruisers and eighteen destroyers.

DID YOU KNOW?

Warships were considerably smaller than during the Second World War, with destroyers having a displacement of well under 1,000 tons and light cruisers being equivalent in size to a Second World War destroyer.

I WAS THERE

I have just lived through the horrible experience of an action at sea, and if there is anyone in the world who having once experienced such an event, says he wishes to experience another, I should not believe him.

Paymaster Hugh Miller, aboard HMS Arethusa at Heligoland Bight, 1914[7]

Alerted by the Admiralty that the Germans were at sea, Sir David Beatty, by now a vice admiral, took his battlecruisers to sea hoping to surprise them. In addition to his flagship HMS *Lion*, Beatty had the *Princess Royal*, *Tiger*, *New Zealand* and *Indomitable*, a far stronger force than Hipper's, and with heavier calibre guns. He also had seven light cruisers and thirty-three destroyers.

Realising the superior strength of the British force, Hipper tried to escape to the south-east, but his ships were steadily overhauled by the British and at 10 a.m., Beatty's ships opened fire at a range of just over 10 miles. *Blücher*, in the rear of the German battle line, was soon hit and began to fall astern of the other ships. *Seydlitz* lost her two aft turrets to a direct hit from the *Lion*, while the *Derfflinger* was also hit, as was the light cruiser *Kolberg*. *Lion* then took three hits, including one below the waterline, and began to fall astern, taking on water and veering out of control. She was hit further before the Germans turned their guns on to *Tiger*, which received several hits and began to burn fiercely. Command was transferred to Rear Admiral Arthur Moore in *New Zealand*, although was never formally assigned as *Lion* had lost her electricity and could not send a wireless signal; furthermore, her signal halyards were blown away and smoke from the fires on board made sending any other kind of signal difficult.

A signal that was sent ordering the other battlecruisers to 'attack the rear of the enemy' was misunderstood and instead of continuing to chase the Germans, the British ships concentrated their fire on the hapless *Blücher*. This was a missed opportunity, as the Germans were down to one operational battlecruiser, the *Moltke*.

Commodore Tyrwhitt then joined the battle with the light cruiser *Arethusa* and four destroyers, which torpedoed the *Blücher*. *Tiger*, which had suffered numerous shell hits,

DID YOU KNOW?

ASDIC, or what is now sonar, did not appear until the end of the war, so hydrophones were used instead. These suffered from interference from the sound of the propellers and machinery of the ships using them. On one occasion, with a ship sitting above a submarine that had been attacked, and which was left on the seabed unable to surface, the crew aboard the ship heard the submarine crew being shot one by one and then the commanding officer taking his own life.

I WAS THERE

We were booming along in the ordinary way and suddenly in the half light saw a row of flashes from the enemy ships. It was a tremendous shock to suddenly see the salvoes dropping all round. They were at extreme range and immediately they saw the battlecruisers turned and ran for their lives. Then we started the chase.

Sub Lieutenant Cyril Bower aboard the destroyer
HMS Laforey at the Battle of Dogger Bank, 1915'

had her fires under control by this time and rejoined the battle. At 11.45 a.m., Moore ordered a ceasefire and shortly after noon *Blücher* rolled over, floated briefly bottom up as her crew scrambled over the hull, and then sank. Out of 1,200 men aboard, just 234 were saved by Tyrwhitt's destroyers. Many of those who died were killed from bombs dropped by a German seaplane that had arrived over the scene with the Zeppelin *L-5*, believing that the British ships were picking up British survivors.

The Germans left the scene of the battle and returned to port, believing, wrongly, that they had sunk the *Tiger*.

BATTLE OF
JUTLAND

THE GREAT NAVAL Battle of Jutland was a defining moment in the First World War at sea. Many believe that it could have been another Trafalgar, and there is little doubt that had it been a great British victory, Germany might have found it difficult to continue the war with the Royal Navy in complete control of the seas. On the other hand, had it been a German victory, Churchill's comment that Jellicoe was 'the only man on either side who could lose the war in an afternoon' would have been fulfilled. That it failed to meet expectations was due to a number of factors that reflected badly on the Admiralty and the commanders involved.

The two opposing fleets were almost mirror images of one another, except that the British Grand Fleet was larger than the German High Seas Fleet. There were two other differences: the Germans were planning to make use of their U-boats to weaken the Grand Fleet before the main battle and the British were using seaplanes for reconnaissance.

DID YOU KNOW?

After Jutland, many naval personnel found themselves booed by dock workers as their ships entered port, so disappointed was the public at the lack of another naval victory to compare with Trafalgar.

I WAS THERE

Noise deafening, and being between the two fleets, we soon felt the heavy shells passing uncomfortably close overhead, even seeing some turning lengthwise over and over. Expecting every moment to be hit and blown to bits, I perched on the foremost torpedo tube, taking a very dim view of events.

Leading Torpedoman P.R. Thorne, aboard the destroyer HMS Nicator, 1916[9]

The Grand Fleet had twenty-eight Dreadnought-standard battleships, nine battlecruisers, eight armoured cruisers, twenty-six light cruisers and seventy-seven destroyers, as well as a seaplane carrier. The High Seas Fleet had sixteen Dreadnought-standard battleships, six pre-Dreadnoughts, five battlecruisers, eleven light cruisers and sixty-one destroyers, as well as a force of U-boats. The Grand Fleet totalled 1,250,000 tons with 60,000 men, while the High Seas Fleet totalled 660,000 tons with 45,000 men.

While the scouting force on both sides had battlecruisers, the Grand Fleet's battlecruiser force also had four of the new Queen Elizabeth-class battleships and the seaplane carrier HMS *Engadine*, a converted Channel packet, as well as light cruisers and destroyers.

Admiral Sir John Jellicoe commanded the Grand Fleet aboard HMS *Iron Duke*, with Vice Admiral David Beatty in his flagship *Lion* heading the battlecruisers, while their opponents were Vice Admiral Reinhard Scheer in his flagship *Friedrich der Grosse* and Vice Admiral Franz von Hipper in his flagship *Lützow*.

On 31 May 1916, the German battlecruisers left harbour at 1 a.m., followed by the main battle fleet at 2.20 a.m. The plan had been for the battleships to provide cover for the battlecruisers in another raid on English towns, in this case the shipbuilding centre of Sunderland. Poor weather had deprived the Grand Fleet of aerial reconnaissance, so Hipper was ordered to take his ships to patrol the Skagerrak, as if threatening British warships and merchant shipping off Norway.

Early in the afternoon, the British light cruiser *Galatea* turned to investigate a Swedish merchantman, just as a German light cruiser did the same. The two ships spotted one another and soon both fleets were on the alert, although neither was aware of the other's presence. At 3.10 p.m., *Engadine* flew off a seaplane on reconnaissance for the first time in naval history.

Decrypted signals by the Admiralty's Room 40 meant that they knew as soon as the *Friedrich der Grosse* left port, but the ship used a different reporting signal when at sea. When Captain Thomas Jackson, the Admiralty's Director of Operations, asked the location of 'DK' – the ship's harbour call sign – he was assured that it was still at Wilhelmshaven because, after leaving, Scheer had the call sign transferred to another ship. Jackson's failure to ask if Scheer, or the *Friedrich der Grosse*, was still in port meant that Jellicoe could not be warned that the High Seas Fleet was heading towards him.

I WAS THERE

All the lights were out, both main and secondary. I managed to get my pad over my face, and those still alive got on the top of the turret, to find the foremost part of the ship blown off, and the after part sinking rapidly. I had got my coat off and one shoe, when the after magazine went up and blew us into the water.

Midshipman J.D. Storey, Q turret aboard HMS Queen Mary, May 1916 [10]

At 3.30 p.m., Hipper's battlecruisers began steering south-east, trying to entice Beatty's ships within range of the High Seas Fleet's battleships. Beatty tried to do the same, and soon the battlecruiser fleets were steaming on a parallel course, with the Grand Fleet to the west. *Lützow* opened fire at 3.48 p.m., with Beatty's ships responding about 3 minutes later.

At 4.05 p.m., *Indefatigable* was sunk by the *Von der Tann* and at 4.25 p.m., shells from *Derfflinger* and *Seydlitz* caused the *Queen Mary* to blow up, as flash from exploding shells penetrated her magazines. Meanwhile, Beatty's four battleships caught up, while both sides deployed destroyers to attack the other with torpedoes.

DID YOU KNOW?

Only Hipper came out of the Battle of Jutland with his reputation intact. Jellicoe and Scheer were both criticised for their tactics, Beatty failed to give Jellicoe the support he needed, and the Admiralty failed to give Jellicoe the information they held about the disposition of the German ships.

The High Seas Fleet battleships appeared at 4.46 p.m., leaving Beatty to try to lure them within range of the Grand Fleet's battleships. He turned north and was chased by the High Seas Fleet, who did not realise that the Grand Fleet was so close. At this stage, a thick mist came down, preventing a continuous engagement. Even so, the light cruiser *Wiesbaden* was caught in the deadly crossfire, followed soon after by the armoured cruiser *Defence*, which blew up. The main fleets clashed at 6.10 p.m., 80 miles west of Jutland. Another British ship, *Warrior*, badly damaged and which would sink the next day, was saved for the time being as *Warspite*'s steering gear jammed and raced around in circles, being hit several times before control was regained.

Shortly afterwards, at 6.33 p.m., *Invincible*, which had been firing well in a gunnery duel with *Derfflinger* and *Lützow*, blew up, although *Lützow* was so badly damaged that she sank the next day.

Jellicoe turned his fleet into the classic line of battle, crossing the enemy's 'T', during which the battleship, *Marlborough*, was struck by a torpedo. Scheer laid a smokescreen hoping that by waiting until dark, the High Seas Fleet could slip away. Nevertheless, the battle continued after dark, with five British destroyers sinking, but the light cruiser *Elbing* sank after being hit by a German battleship, while another light cruiser, *Rostock*, was torpedoed and sunk and the pre-Dreadnought, *Pommern*, was torpedoed and exploded. The armoured cruiser, *Black Prince*, sank under heavy fire. By noon, the Germans were back in their ports and the Grand Fleet was back in its ports by the end of the day.

The Royal Navy lost three battlecruisers, three armoured cruisers, eight destroyers and the lives of 6,090 men. The Imperial German Navy lost a battleship and a pre-Dreadnought, four light cruisers and five destroyers, with the lives of 2,550 men. On paper it was a German victory, but Jellicoe had saved the Grand Fleet and retained control of the seas.

SUBMARINES IN THE BALTIC

MOST PEOPLE HAVE heard of the threat posed by the German U-boats, which at one time threatened to bring the UK to its knees through starvation. What is less widely known is the part played by British submariners in both the Baltic and the Sea of Marmara. The skill and determination, as well as the courage of the submariners lay not simply in what they achieved in both these largely enclosed seas, but in their ability to get their submarines into these operational zones in the first place.

At the outset of the war, many had thought that a fleet could be sent into the Baltic to carry the war to the enemy, with an invasion of Germany through Pomerania, mainly using Russian troops, bringing an early end to the conflict. This, of course, overlooked the difficulties of navigating large ships through the Skagerrak and the Kattegat and the increasing instability in Russia. Nevertheless, the Germans were already demonstrating the potential of the submarine, forcing the Grand Fleet to move from Scapa Flow to Loch Ewe and Lough Swilly.

The idea of a submarine campaign in the Baltic had first been discussed with Jellicoe aboard HMS *Iron Duke* on 17 September 1914. The plan was for a flotilla of submarines, but this was eventually reduced to just three boats: *E11* with Lieutenant Commander Martin

Nasmith, E9 with Lieutenant Commander Max Horton, and E1 with Lieutenant Commander Noel Laurence, who was the senior officer. The problem was that there was insufficient depth of water for submarines to pass submerged through the Kattegat between Denmark and Sweden. Therefore, Horton proposed running through the Kattegat on the surface, but with the submarine trimmed as low as possible so that only the conning tower was above the water.

E1 and E9 left Gorleston just after dark on 15 October, leaving E11 behind, as her engines would not start. The following day, E9 suffered a broken shaft and fell behind as she was being repaired. That afternoon, E1 entered the Skagerrak after dark, diving each time a surface vessel approached, and waited on the seabed the following day before attempting the passage of the Kattegat. That night, E1 made a successful passage through the Kattegat and was in the Baltic by midnight. E9 was doing her best to catch up, but a succession of surface vessels in the Skagerrak had meant she had to submerge most of the time. Dawn on 17 October found the two submarines submerged at opposite ends of the Kattegat.

On 18 October, E1 started her first patrol of the Baltic. At periscope depth, Laurence spotted a German cruiser and fired a torpedo, which ran too deep, but alerted the crew so that the ship managed to evade a second torpedo. Alerted, the Germans intensified their patrols in the Kattegat so that Horton only just managed to get through.

After failing to find targets in Danzig harbour, Laurence took *E1* to Libau (now Liepaja) in Latvia, to be told he had just passed through a German minefield. Worse, the speed of the German advance meant that he would have to use Lappvik as a base, but had to wait for *E9* to arrive, as he had no means of communication.

E11 by this time had made two attempts to pass through the Kattegat, but the first was foiled by intensive German patrols, and on the second occasion Nasmith nearly torpedoed a neutral

DID YOU KNOW?

The Russians objected when Horton and Laurence were recalled. They then suggested that Horton become the Senior Naval Officer Baltic, but the Second Sea Lord turned this down because Horton 'was something of a pirate'. He became Commander-in-Chief, Western Approaches, during the Second World War, responsible for protecting Allied shipping from U-boats.

I WAS THERE

In my opinion the moral courage displayed by Nasmith in giving up his attempt to pass through the Sound [the Kattegat] was as admirable as the bravery and enterprise which won him the Victoria Cross in the Marmara later.

Roger Keyes, commodore in charge of submarines, commenting on Lieutenant Commander Martin Nasmith's failed operation in the Baltic, October 1914 [11]

Danish submarine; therefore, on 22 October, he gave up and returned to Gorleston.

The enemy was not the only problem they faced. The Baltic was beginning to freeze over and *E9* needed an icebreaker to get out of port and into the open sea. Once in the open sea, spray froze on the vents and rigging and valves froze solid. Fortunately, on trying to see if she could still dive, Horton found that the warmer water thawed the ice. The rest of the winter was spent sheltering from the weather, and the Germans.

E1 and *E9* resumed their campaign in spring 1915. They followed the prize rules, boarding German merchant ships and allowing those aboard to take to the lifeboats before the ship was sunk. *E9* was sent to attack enemy troopships returning to Danzig, sinking one when a torpedo struck amidships. In calm water, however, whenever Horton raised his periscope, he was spotted and cruisers and destroyers fired at the submarine. The Germans did not have depth charges, but they used an explosive charge on the end of a sweep that worked very well in shallow waters. Later, Horton in *E9* sank a destroyer and a collier.

Convinced that an entire submarine flotilla was loose in the Baltic, the Germans suspended all shipping movements. On 2 July,

I WAS THERE

I consider the destruction of a Russian submarine will be a great success, but I regard the destruction of a British submarine as being at least as valuable as that of a Russian armoured cruiser.

Prince Henry of Prussia, German Commander-in-Chief of the Baltic fleet[12]

DID YOU KNOW?

The Russian Navy was the first of that country's armed forces to be taken over by the Bolsheviks. It played little part in the war, although the British plan for an invasion of Germany through Pomerania believed that the Russians would provide most of the manpower.

some shipping was moving again and Horton fired two torpedoes that put the cruiser *Prinz Adalbert* out of action for four months – his torpedoes were too small to sink a larger ship.

With such success from just two submarines, the Admiralty decided to reinforce the operation. Four more E-class submarines were sent as well as four of the older and smaller C-class, which were towed to Archangel and then reached Petrograd by way of rivers and canals, and much manual labour. A number of ships were sunk by the enlarged force, including a steamer and an ore carrier, and damage was inflicted on the battlecruiser *Moltke*, forcing Hipper to reverse course. On 22 October, *E8* sank the cruiser *Prinz Adalbert* when a torpedo penetrated her magazine, blowing her up. On one day, no less than five ships were sunk.

E13 ran aground and was in danger of being interned, but broke free only to be attacked in Danish waters by two German torpedo boats. On fire, she was abandoned by her crew, many of whom either drowned or were machine-gunned in the water by the Germans until a Danish destroyer was put between them and the Germans.

The campaign was resumed in spring 1916, but the advance of the Germans and the unrest that preceded the Russian Revolution meant that it was drawing to an end. The Germans had in any case discovered an effective anti-submarine weapon in the depth charge.

THE DARDANELLES

HAVING REALISED THAT any landings in the Baltic would be all but impossible, the British Government turned its attention to landings on the Gallipoli Peninsula and to forcing the Dardanelles. While the Dardanelles and the associated ground campaign in Gallipoli was a disaster, the one success story that comes from this tragic waste of manpower and opportunity was that of the submarine service.

While Turkey and the United Kingdom had been on good terms for many years, a number of disagreements and successful German wooing of the Turks before the outbreak of the First World War meant that relations were strained. They were strained further on 3 August 1914 when the news came that the Turks were laying mines in the Dardanelles. The following day, the

DID YOU KNOW?

The Royal Navy's use of the submarine was inhibited by the belief that they were the best means of countering other submarines, rather than the ideal way of attacking surface shipping. One reason for this was that warships of any kind tackling a merchant ship were supposed to board, and allow the crew and any passengers to leave before sinking it.

I WAS THERE

16.00 Rose to the surface, and by going full speed astern, and rising to the surface stern first, managed to shake clear a large mine which had been hanging to the port foremost hydroplane since passing Chanak.

Lieutenant Commander Martin Nasmith in command of E11, the Dardanelles, 1915[13]

UK's declaration of war on Germany saw two German warships – the battlecruiser *Goeben* and her escort, the cruiser *Breslau*, that had been returning from Turkey – change course and head back to Constantinople, transferring with their crews to the Turkish Navy and being renamed as *Sultan Selim* and *Medilli* respectively. Despite provocation by the Turks, the UK did not declare war on Turkey until 5 November 1914, but had earlier rejected offers of assistance against Turkey by the Greek Government.

Inaction before the declaration of war would have been understandable, but what followed was a rash misjudgement. First Lord of the Admiralty Winston Churchill ignored advice to land an army at Gallipoli while the Turks were unprepared and instead ordered battleships to bombard the forts of the lower Dardanelles. This alerted the Turks and their German allies to British interest in the area and gave them time to organise strong defences.

On 13 December 1914, the elderly British submarine *B11* sneaked past the Dardanelles minefields and sunk the battlecruiser *Messudieh*, for which Lieutenant Holbrook, the commanding officer, received the Victoria Cross. As part of a sustained campaign, this could have done much to weaken Turkish resistance, but as a solitary action, all it did was put the Turks on the alert.

The next plan of action was to land on Gallipoli. This was to be the ground action, started on 25 April 1915, but it was ill conceived, with poor intelligence about Turkish troop dispositions, the terrain or the likely weather conditions and Turkish fighting ability was underestimated. Worst of all, the Admiralty and the War Office did not support the plan, with the latter providing commanders who were not regarded as good enough for the Western Front, and causing difficulties over supplies, while Lord Fisher at the Admiralty would only allocate obsolete warships.

Apart from coastal bombardment, the Royal Navy's role was to deliver floating pontoons for the landings, but regarded this work as beneath them, subcontracting the role to merchant shipping, who abandoned seven of the eight piers in the Mediterranean and left the eighth offshore on the island of Lemnos. Members of the Royal Naval Air Service flew reconnaissance and light bombing missions, but it was not until the evacuation, ordered on 10 December 1915, that surface units of the Royal Navy became heavily involved, taking 134,000 British and Empire troops so efficiently that by the New Year just 40,000 remained ashore – these were taken off on the night of 8/9 January 1916.

DID YOU KNOW?

To counter German merchant raiders, the British deployed merchant ships known as 'Q' ships, with concealed guns which were exposed to challenge the raider, but before this a 'panic party' would take to the lifeboats to persuade the German raider that all was well and the British ship could be sunk.

THE SUBMARINE CAMPAIGN

Meanwhile, the Royal Navy, encouraged by the success of *B11*, had sent more submarines to the Sea of Marmara. The Turks responded by moving their ships out of the Dardanelles to Constantinople. Four E-class boats were sent to the Aegean, and these, unlike the B-class, could reach Constantinople.

On 17 April 1915, the first attempt was a failure due to a strong current that swept *E15* ashore, with the crew escaping to be taken prisoner by the Turks, while the Royal Naval Air Service and ships of the Dardanelles Squadron attempted to destroy her. The Australian *AE2* was next, but also failed to run through the Dardanelles, although at least she returned. Unfortunately, she was lost later.

I WAS THERE

We shelled a railway and destroyed two troop trains. We shelled the embankment and blocked the line, and then caught the trains as [they] came along. It was the funniest thing you can imagine to see the trains try to hide behind trees. But we caught them and smashed them to blazes.

Sub Lieutenant I.M. Twyman aboard E7 [14]

It was on 27 April that *E14*, commanded by Lieutenant Commander Edward Boyle, reached the Sea of Marmara, taking seventeen hours for the passage through the Dardanelles, sixteen hours of which were submerged. Boyle found and sank a torpedo gunboat with his second torpedo. Boyle afterwards found difficulty in finding somewhere to surface in order to recharge his batteries, but the submarine patrols were intensified. He sunk a second gunboat on 1 May, while the Turks had to reroute their troop movements over land. Lacking a deck armament, Boyle surfaced and exchanged gunfire with troops. On 10 May, he sank the troopship *Guj Djemal*, carrying no less than 6,000 troops. On 13 May, he used a rifle to force a small steamer to run aground. After this, Boyle was to make two more successful excursions into the Marmara.

Next was Lieutenant Commander Martin Nasmith with *E11* on 19 May, who had been flown on a reconnaissance mission over the area. The havoc he created was even worse than that of *E14*. He convinced the Turks that a whole flotilla was in the area, sinking a large gunboat, an ammunition ship, three store ships and two transports, as well as four minor vessels including a troop-carrying barge. He also made two further visits to the Marmara.

Other submarines engaged in these actions included *E2* and *E7*. Nevertheless, with the Gallipoli campaign abandoned and attention turning to the defence of Greece, the Royal Navy's priorities turned elsewhere.

BASES

HISTORICALLY, THE ROYAL Navy's main enemy over several centuries was the French, and so the main naval bases were in the south of England, at Plymouth (more usually known as Devonport), Portsmouth and Chatham (also known as the Nore). Even when the Spanish, and later the Dutch, became the enemies, these bases were still well placed. Chatham existed to defend London and both Chatham and Portsmouth were major shipbuilding yards, with HMS *Dreadnought* being built at the latter.

As tensions rose and Germany became the most likely enemy in any war, the traditional bases were far too far away. This was a problem, as the east coast of Scotland offered few natural bases, especially with dockyard facilities, and the further north the base, the poorer the surface communications. A sheltered anchorage was also important, but so too was easy access to the sea.

DID YOU KNOW?

For the Grand Fleet based at Scapa Flow, coal had to be carried by train from South Wales to Grangemouth, on the south shore of the Firth of Forth, where it was transferred to a ship for Scapa. The trains were known as 'Jellicoe Specials' and 13,630 were run between August 1914 and March 1919.

I WAS THERE

I wonder if we will still be here in the morning.

Admiral Sir John Jellicoe to a visiting admiral at Scapa Flow, referring to the U-boat menace[15]

In the search for a suitable location, the choice was Rosyth, on the north bank of the Firth of Forth and close to Edinburgh by rail. This was, nevertheless, an unpopular choice with many senior officers as Rosyth was some distance from the open sea, with few opportunities for gunnery practise, and ships had to pass under the Forth Bridge, carrying the railway line to Aberdeen and the north of Scotland. Construction work began in 1909 and continued at a leisurely pace until the dockyard was opened by King George V in June 1915, by which time the nation was already at war with Germany. In fact, the base was not operationally ready until 1916.

Unlike Devonport, Portsmouth or Chatham, Rosyth was not a manning port. After the First World War, a good indication of official attitudes towards Rosyth was that it was closed until 1939. During the First World War, it was used by the Grand Fleet's battlecruisers, which were as likely to be ordered south to defend the ports on the Humber as they were north.

The other base on the east coast of Scotland was at Invergordon on the Cromarty Firth. This was a good sheltered anchorage with the drawback that the entrance was narrow and easy to block, while road and rail access from the south was along a single-tracked line, steeply graded in places. However, it was close to the sea and, while at the Admiralty before the war, Jellicoe managed to get a large floating dock placed near Invergordon, reducing the need for major fleet units to make the long voyage south. This was used extensively by the Royal Navy's cruisers, but was probably not big enough for battleships and battlecruisers.

Further north still, north of the Scottish mainland, Scapa Flow was not so much a base as an anchorage. Located on the south coast of the mainland of Orkney, the big advantage was its proximity to Germany, which meant that it was ideal for the blockade. Its vast size meant that almost any fleet could be accommodated and much training could take place in its sheltered waters. There were big drawbacks, however. It lacked any kind of repair facility or railway connection, so that men and supplies had to come by sea, and it was so large that enormous waves could sweep across it – it was not unknown for men to be washed overboard into the sea. Furthermore, there were many entrances, which made security a problem. At the height of the U-boat scare, Jellicoe took the Grand Fleet away to a base at Loch Ewe on the west coast of Scotland, and to Lough Swilly in County Donegal on the north coast of Ireland. Lough Swilly was not particularly safe, as the Dreadnought HMS *Audacious* was sunk after hitting a mine off nearby Londonderry on 27 October 1914.

To prepare Scapa Flow before the war, a small headquarters was established ashore and the repair ships *Assistance* and *Cyclops* moored off the pier, with a telegraph cable running from *Cyclops* to Kirkwall and on to the mainland of Scotland and then down to the Admiralty in London. Defensive measures included putting the two elderly pre-Dreadnought battleships *Hannibal* and *Magnificent*, with 12in guns, at the two main entrances, while shore batteries of 4in and 6in guns were also established. Submarine defences were basic, with nets strung between buoys in the main channel, and after these proved unable to cope with the winter weather, herring drifters were converted with stronger and heavier nets strung between them. Fifty armed trawlers patrolled the entrances, towing explosive sweeps, and defensive minefields were laid. It took until May 1915 before these measures were completed. Before this, on 24 November 1914, a submarine attempting to enter Scapa Flow was rammed by an armed trawler and was eventually scuttled, with the crew taken prisoner. The minefield was activated to sink *UB-116* late on 28 October 1918: there were no survivors.

I WAS THERE

Fortunately, we were spared the unpleasantness of being hissed by our countrymen as we went to Scapa Flow where there were only heather-covered islands to greet us.

Midshipman R.H.C.F. Frampton on returning to Scapa Flow after Jutland in 1916 [16]

DID YOU KNOW?

Scapa, Invergordon and Rosyth were all desperately needed because for centuries Great Britain's potential foes had been across the English Channel or the Bay of Biscay. Germany had not been seen as a threat, partly because it did not become a unified nation until the late nineteenth century.

A number of other bases were established around the coast of England. Dover, the main Continental packet port, was closed to civilian traffic on the outbreak of war to enable the British Expeditionary Force to be moved to France and Belgium. The need to re-supply the British Expeditionary Force and protect its supply line meant that the port remained in naval hands for the rest of the war and acted as the base for the Dover Patrol, created to counter enemy attacks and prevent mine laying, as well as closing the Straits of Dover to German warships.

Harwich, another packet port especially for travellers to the Netherlands, was also used for warships guarding the approach to the Thames Estuary and for offensive operations against German North Sea ports. Two flotillas were based at Harwich: one for submarines, commanded by Commodore (later Rear Admiral) Roger Keyes, and the other for destroyers commanded by Commodore (later Rear Admiral) Reginald Tyrwhitt. Both 'flotillas' were often more than one flotilla strong.

GERMAN
COASTAL RAIDS

GUNNERY HAD REACHED such a level that attacks on coastal targets had become an attractive proposition for an enemy. Much of the Royal Navy's active duty in the North Sea was originally intended to deter a German invasion of Great Britain, but at no time did the Germans consider such a move.

Maintaining a watch on the North Sea was costly, and this fact was brought home on 22 September 1914, when three elderly British armoured cruisers, *Aboukir*, *Cressy* and *Hogue*, were all torpedoed and sunk by *U-9* within the space of just one hour. Many criticised the Admiralty for allowing such substantial ships so close to waters in which the enemy was likely to be present.

There could be no attempt at fortifying the entire east coast of England, and despite the best efforts of the Dover patrol and the flotillas at Harwich, as well as estuarial patrols on the Forth and Humber, there were inevitably weak spots in the defences. In addition, during the war, the Royal Navy decided, rightly, that the southern North Sea was no place for its largest ships, due to the many shallows and the danger of being boxed in by enemy forces. The Imperial German Navy, on the other hand, saw the area as being vulnerable to fast-moving battlecruisers on what might be described as 'hit and run' raids.

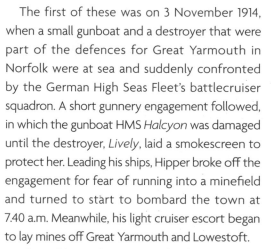

DID YOU KNOW?

Radio reception aboard submarines at the time was so poor that when they put to sea in flotilla strength, one or two destroyers were sent as escorts to pass messages on to the submarines, with the destroyers receiving the radio messages and then signalling the submarines.

The first of these was on 3 November 1914, when a small gunboat and a destroyer that were part of the defences for Great Yarmouth in Norfolk were at sea and suddenly confronted by the German High Seas Fleet's battlecruiser squadron. A short gunnery engagement followed, in which the gunboat HMS *Halcyon* was damaged until the destroyer, *Lively*, laid a smokescreen to protect her. Leading his ships, Hipper broke off the engagement for fear of running into a minefield and turned to start to bombard the town at 7.40 a.m. Meanwhile, his light cruiser escort began to lay mines off Great Yarmouth and Lowestoft.

Alerted by *Halcyon*'s signals, the remaining four destroyers and three submarines at Great Yarmouth got ready to put to sea. Only one of them, *D5*, got close to the Germans, but then struck a mine and, with the exception of two officers and two men in her conning tower, all aboard perished.

I WAS THERE

16.00 Signal 'All German flotillas have been warned to be ready for service tonight'. This was a 'tapped' wireless message. We have their code – the Russians collared it some time ago from a ship that went ashore and of course gave it to us.

Sub Lieutenant P.W. Bowyer-Smyth aboard HMS Superb [17]

The Admiralty had known that the Germans were at sea as early as 7 a.m., but it was not until 9.55 a.m. that Beatty was ordered to pursue the raiders with his battlecruisers, but by that time it was too late and Hipper's force was on its way back to Wilhelmshaven. It was fortunate that his shells had landed either in the sea or on a deserted beach. The minefield accounted for a submarine and three trawlers, but by a quirk of fate, one of Hipper's armoured cruisers was sunk in Wilhelmshaven's protective minefield with the loss of more than 200 men.

Hipper tried again on 15 December 1914, with four battlecruisers and an armoured cruiser, as well as four light cruisers for mine laying and eighteen destroyers. It was followed in the afternoon by the rest of the High Seas Fleet, ready to intervene should the Royal Navy attempt to cut off the battlecruisers. Severe weather caused Hipper to order the light cruisers and destroyers back to join the High Seas Fleet, with the exception of the mine-laying cruiser. The force was divided into two, with two ships sent to Scarborough plus the light cruiser, which was to lay mines off Flamborough Head. Hipper took the remaining three ships to Hartlepool.

DID YOU KNOW?

The early submarines used petrol engines to provide propulsion while on the surface and also to recharge their batteries, but this fuel was highly explosive and dangerous. By the First World War, the best submarines, such as the E-class, had diesel engines, which used a much safer fuel.

On 16 December, at 8 a.m., Scarborough was shaken by heavy gunfire, with shells crashing into the town centre. In thirty minutes, seventeen people were killed and another ninety-nine wounded. Next, Hipper's ships opened fire on the fishing port of Whitby, but this bombardment lasted just ten minutes, leaving two dead and another two wounded.

At Hartlepool, four elderly destroyers were at sea and at 7.46 a.m. warned those ashore that three unidentified warships were approaching. As the German ships opened fire, three of the destroyers turned back, but one, HMS *Doon*, continued towards the battlecruisers under heavy fire, launching a torpedo, which missed its target, before turning back with one man dead and another eleven wounded.

I WAS THERE

I met a ship once that didn't 'smell' right for me, and remained five kilometres distant, fired a shot across his bow and signalled 'send a boat with your papers'. The boat came only a little way across and stopped. They were trying to get me to come closer. I fired again, and at that the boat made a run for it, and the British had it back on board and were off. I fired on them but they got away.

Franz Becker, U-boat commanding officer[18]

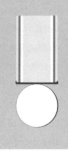

The shelling of Hartlepool started at 8.10 a.m., with the first falling on an artillery position, killing seven men and wounding eleven. A light cruiser and a submarine tried to put to sea, but the former had to be run aground to save her, as she was hit by heavy shells of up to 11in, while the submarine grounded. The bombardment ended at 8.52 a.m. after 1,150 shells were fired at the town, killing eighty-six civilians as well as the gunners, and no less than 424 wounded.

The submarine at Hartlepool was supposed to be at sea in case German warships appeared. At Harwich, submarines and destroyers put to sea, while Jellicoe sent battlecruisers and armoured cruisers south to try to block Hipper's passage home. At 5.15 a.m. on 16 December, a gunnery exchange started between a German ship and seven British destroyers, but two of the British ships were so badly damaged that they had to turn back. Shortly afterwards, the British destroyer spotted the German light cruiser *Hamburg* and came under fire, with HMS *Hardy* set on fire, but even so, she managed to fire a torpedo, which missed, but caused the *Hamburg* to turn for home.

The Admiralty ordered Jellicoe to take the Grand Fleet south to engage the Germans, but they were too far north at Scapa Flow to reach the enemy in time. Nevertheless, the spirited

resistance by the British destroyers persuaded
the Germans that they had come too far west
for safety.

CORONEL AND
THE FALKLANDS

SHORTLY AFTER THE outbreak of war, the Admiralty sent its older ships to the more distant parts of the empire to watch for German surface raiders. The best ships were kept at home, concentrated in keeping a blockade of German ports and guarding against a German invasion.

One role for the ships that were so widely dispersed was to protect troopships bringing men from the empire to fight in Europe. In September 1914, the Royal Navy escorted 50,000 men being moved from India to the UK, while another 25,000 men were escorted from Canada across the Atlantic in October and in November 26,000 troops came from Australia and New Zealand. Reluctance to introduce convoys in northern waters did not stop the Royal Navy from running convoys in the Pacific and Indian Oceans.

An idea of how great was the threat posed by the commerce raiders can be gained from the fact that just two ships, *Emden* and *Karlsruhe*, sank thirty-nine merchant ships, accounting for 176,000 tons of merchant shipping. *Emden* was disguised as a four-funnelled British light cruiser, but gained some respect for the way in which the crews and any passengers aboard merchant ships were allowed to leave before they were sunk. Nevertheless, she was eventually spotted, reported and then tracked down by the Australian light cruiser *Sydney*.

DID YOU KNOW?

Vice Admiral Sturdee was sent to the South Atlantic because the First Sea Lord wanted to punish him for spreading the Royal Navy's warships too thinly. The irony was that in preparing to counter Spee, this is just what Fisher was forced to do, spreading the available ships more thinly.

Coronel

Not all of the German operations on the Pacific and elsewhere were by ships disguised as British warships or merchant vessels. A German battle squadron was also loose in the Pacific, the German East Asiatic Squadron, based on Tsingtao in China. This was commanded by Admiral von Spee and had the two armoured cruisers *Scharnhorst* and *Gneisenau*, as well as two light cruisers and an armed merchant cruiser.

Sailing down the coast of South America on his way to rendezvous with the cruisers of the German American Station, Spee encountered Rear Admiral Sir Christopher Cradock, who had taken part of his squadron around Cape Horn looking for Spee's squadron. Cradock only had the armoured cruisers *Good Hope* and *Monmouth*, both obsolete, the new light cruiser *Glasgow* and the armed merchant cruiser *Otranto*.

On 1 November 1914, the two forces met in bad weather off the Chilean coast near Coronel. In the high seas, only the armoured cruisers were able to use their guns effectively, but the two elderly British ships were silenced quickly, with *Good Hope* sinking after an hour, and Cradock became the first of four British admirals to lose his life in a naval battle during the war. *Monmouth* was torpedoed and sank with no survivors, but their sacrifice allowed *Glasgow* and *Otranto* to escape.

DID YOU KNOW?

Foreign powers placing warship orders with British yards had to agree to a contract that allowed the Royal Navy to keep the ship if needed. This was one reason for Turkey siding with Germany and Austro-Hungary, as warships for Turkey were retained by the British. This was not a means of getting foreign powers to pay for the upkeep of the Royal Navy as no further payment was expected, and replacement warships were built for the customer later.

I WAS THERE

We turned and ran. We reluctantly said goodbye to her [Monmouth] ... it was suicide to follow as the enemy were concentrating their fire on us. They missed us in the dark.

Lieutenant Commander P.J. Shrubsole, aboard HMS Glasgow at Coronel, 1914[19]

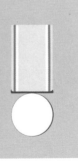

I WAS THERE

At 09.00 two ships came close to Port William where we were coaling. The Canopus – the ship stationed at Port Stanley – fired on them. The ships made off at once.

Midshipman A.G. McEwan, aboard Invincible, December 1914[20]

Falkland Islands

It took three days for the news of the defeat at Coronel to reach the Admiralty, and then it came from German sources, boasting of their victory.

The problem was that Spee's ships could round Cape Horn and start to attack ships bringing food from the Argentine and Uruguay to the UK, but on the other hand, they could go through the Panama Canal and engage the West Indies Squadron. There were other possibilities as well in Africa. The battlecruiser *Princess Royal* was sent to the West Indies to reinforce the squadron there. The battlecruisers *Invincible* and *Inflexible* were ordered to Devonport to prepare for service overseas, while the elderly pre-Dreadnought battleship *Canopus* was ordered to ground herself on the approaches to Port Stanley to act as a fort.

Under the command of Vice Admiral Doveton Sturdee, the ships reached Port Stanley on 7 December 1914 after rendezvousing with the South Atlantic Squadron commanded by Rear Admiral Stoddart. Coaling began immediately, but the battlecruisers waited until the following morning so that some ships were available to fight. The battlecruisers had started coaling at 5.30 a.m. on 8 December but was interrupted at 9 a.m. as the guns of *Canopus* opened fire on two approaching warships. Coaling stopped immediately and steam raised, with Sturdee's ships leaving the harbour at 10 a.m.

The two ships had been the armoured cruiser *Gneisenau* and the light cruiser *Nürnberg*, which had been unaware of the British battlecruisers and turned and raced back to rejoin *Scharnhorst*, which had Spee aboard.

At 1 p.m. the first shells started to fall on the German ships, causing Spee to divide his forces, hoping that by sacrificing *Scharnhorst* and *Gneisenau*, the light cruisers could escape. The Germans were outgunned, facing the 12in guns of the battlecruisers with 8in guns, and their lower calibre guns also had a shorter range so they came under fire before they could return it. At 4.15 p.m., *Scharnhorst* went down with all hands and at 6 p.m. *Gneisenau* followed.

Sturdee had also divided his forces, sending his light cruisers after the German ships. HMS *Kent* caught and sank the *Nürnberg*, while *Glasgow* and *Cornwall* caught and sank the *Leizig*.

IMPACT OF THE
WAR AT SEA

AN ISLAND NATION, the British were not unused to Continental wars, but nevertheless saw themselves as a maritime power, and with good reason. They not only had the world's largest navy in 1914, but they also had the largest merchant navy and carried 43 per cent of the world's seaborne trade in their ships.

They had two priorities. The first was to ensure that the nation's trade was protected and the second was to blockade Germany. The Royal Navy came close to failing on the first requirement by not introducing a convoy system until 1918 and in the meantime the nation came perilously close to starvation. Nevertheless, U-boat and surface raider alike were hunted down and the main trade routes kept open.

The blockade of Germany worked and by 1918 the Germans were facing an increasing shortage of food, animal feed and fertiliser, while the High Seas Fleet was still outnumbered and outgunned by the Grand Fleet. It was the increasingly desperate situation on the German home front more than anything else, not even the arrival of the first American troops, that began to tip the balance and finally allow the Allies to advance.

Surrender did not come immediately, for the Armistice on 11 November 1918 was just that and in theory hostilities could have resumed, but only in theory, as most of the High Seas Fleet was moved to Scapa Flow – a humiliation for the Imperial German Navy. Most of the ships that arrived at Scapa Flow were scuttled on 21 June 1919, exactly a week before the Treaty of Versailles was signed, which marked the formal end to the war.

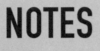

NOTES

1   Imperial War Museum Sound Archive.
2   Ibid.
3   Padfield, Peter, *Dönitz – The Last Führer, Portrait of a Nazi War Leader* (Victor Gollancz, 1984).
4   Ibid.
5   Imperial War Museum Sound Archive.
6   Imperial War Museum Sound Archive.
7   Ibid.
8   Ibid.
9   Ibid.
10 Ibid.
11 Ibid.
12 Ibid.
13 Ibid.
14 Ibid.
15 Ibid.
16 Ibid.
17 Ibid.
18 Ibid.
19 Ibid.
20 Ibid.

BIBLIOGRAPHY

Gray, Edwyn, *British Submarines in the Great War* (Pen & Sword, 2001).

Massie, Robert K., *Castles of Steel, Britain, Germany and the Winning of the Great War at Sea* (Jonathan Cape, 2004).

Thompson, Julian, *The Imperial War Museum Book of the War at Sea, 1914–1918* (Sidgwick & Jackson, 2005).

Wragg, David, *Royal Navy Handbook 1914–1918* (Sutton, 2006).

Discover more books in this series ...

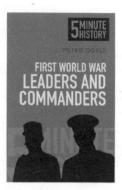

978-0-7509-5570-6   £5.00

978-0-7509-5571-3   £5.00

978-0-7524-9322-0   £5.00

978-0-7524-9321-3   £5.00

Visit our website and discover thousands
of other History Press books.

www.thehistorypress.co.uk